GUIDED PRAYERS FOR EVERY ASPECT
OF YOUR WRITING JOURNEY

Prayers FOR Writers

TARA G. ERICSON

Copyright 2022
Silver Fountain Press, LLC
All Rights Reserved.

Scripture quotations are from the ESV® Bible
(The Holy Bible, English Standard Version®),
copyright © 2001 by Crossway Bibles,
a publishing ministry of Good News Publishers.
Used by permission. All rights reserved.

Table of Contents

Prayers for a Writer's Heart

Calling 7
Equipping 11
Priorities 15
Personal Faith 19
Worship 23
Humility 27
Obedience 31
My Heart 35

Prayers for My Writing

Creativity 41
Creating with God 45
Learning 49
Boldness 53
Message 57
Reader's Hearts 61

Prayers for My Circle

My Partner 67
My Children 71
My Friendships 75
My Writer Friends 79
My Teachers 83
My Writing Team 87
My Prayer Team 91

Prayers for a Writing Business

Decisions   97
Finances   101
Success   105
Platform   109
Reputation   113
Technology   117
Opportunities   121
Time Management   125

Prayers for Specific Times

Starting a New Project   131
Morning Writing   133
Afternoon Writing   135
Evening Writing   137
Writer's Block   139
Editing   141
Finishing a Project   143
Release & Publication   145
Rejection   147
Anxiety   149
Waiting   151
Comparison   153

Dear Writer

I don't know where you are on your journey, or what you write. But if you are a follower of Christ, then I do know something. I know that the most powerful tool in your writer's toolbox isn't strong verbs, fast dictation, or a 21-page character profile. It's not a new laptop or the perfect notebook with the ideal line spacing.

It's prayer.

As I've spent the better part of five years transitioning from my day job as a corporate sales engineer and recruiter to a journey I never expected as an author of Christian fiction, the only constant thing has been God's constant grace, guidance, and provision.

As you go through this book, I hope you'll find the same thing. I know that God deeply desires to be invited into your writing, and that if you cover it in prayer, your writing will flourish in ways you never expected.

Perhaps you, like me, feel a call to write that you never expected. Or perhaps you have always been a writer. Either way, rest in the assurance that God has a plan for your writing and can use it in big and small ways to transform you and the world.

Whether you spend sixty hours a week writing, or six minutes jotting notes down about an idea, this book is for you, writer. Whatever your genre, whether poetry or non-fiction or mystery novels or romances, this book is for you.

Within these pages, you'll find prayers on topics related to your writing craft, your faith, the people in your life, and prayers for specific times in your writing journey.

I encourage you to use the empty spaces to reflect on the questions and write prayers of your own. We are writers, after all.

Dear writer, the God in heaven above loves you with an everlasting love. He rejoices when you use the gifts he has given you! I hope these pages will help you invite your Creator into this special piece of your heart and life.

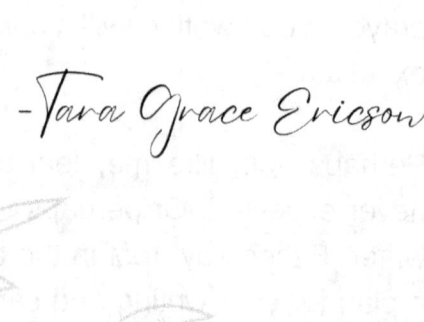

-Tara Grace Ericson

My Prayer for You

Generous, loving Father,

Meet my friend here in these pages. As they draw near to you, fill them with your holy presence. Let their time in prayer be sacred time. Bless their time with few interruptions from the demands of the day.

While they meet you here, show them new and wonderful things, Lord, about the gift you have given them. Fill them with new understanding of how they can use this unique gifting to benefit your kingdom. Fill them with a desire to please you with their words, whatever they may write.

Draw these writers close, Lord. Protect them from depression, anxiety, comparison, self-doubt, fear, or spiritual attacks. When they are assailed with such things, remind them of your good and gracious purpose for their lives and your eternal love and perfect joy.

Instead, fill them with peace, confidence, boldness, joy, and excitement about their writing. Give them a hunger to write and motivation to complete the tasks you have called them to.

Assure them of your complete pleasure in them, Lord, that they may find their validation, purpose, and identity in you and you alone.

Renew a passion for writing inside them, Lord. And use these prayers and their time with you to encourage, strengthen, and build them up.

Thank you for their gift. May it be a blessing to you, to them, their families, and to all who read their words. What a marvelous creator you are to gift us so uniquely and generously! We praise you for we are fearfully and wonderfully made: as writers, as well as brothers and sisters, and mothers and fathers, daughters and sons.

I praise you, O Lord that you will accomplish more than they could ask or imagine as they write as worship with obedience, and a tender heart. I praise you that they are here, eager to meet with you and invite you in.

In your precious and Holy name,

Amen

*And now, go, write it before them on a tablet
and inscribe it in a book, that it may be
for the time to come as a witness forever.*

Isaiah 30:8

Prayers for a Writer's Heart

"No matter what people tell you, words and ideas can change the world."

Robin Williams

Calling

Father God,

I thank you for this gift, this special calling that you have placed in my life. It is a great treasure to be a writer, Lord! You are the great author, using words to share your heart with the world. So I strive to do, humbly, in a reflection of your image.

Throughout scripture, you call those the world would overlook. The "least of these," you elevate to the highest places of honor. I offer myself, inadequate and unworthy, to be used by you through the words I write.

When I question my call as a writer, I ask for your gentle reminder. Let me never doubt that you created me to be a creator myself.

Sometimes, Lord, I don't feel like I'm "called" to write. Help me see how you have purposefully gifted me with this skill and this desire to write. Help me recognize that my desire to write comes from you.

Where you have called me to serve in other ways, help me to remain faithful to each.

Scripture

1 Thess 5:24
*For the one who called you is faithful,
he will surely do it.*

2 Peter 1:10
Therefore, brothers, be all the more diligent to confirm your calling and election, for if you practice these qualities you will never fall.

Ephesians 2:10
For we are his workmanship, created in Christ Jesus for good works, which God prepared beforehand, that we should walk in them.

Respond

Spend time thanking God for calling you to write.

_____
_____
_____
_____
_____
_____
_____

In what ways has the Lord affirmed your writing?

Do you feel worthy of the call he's given you?

Is there a call from the Lord that you have not yet responded to? Pray about your next steps.

Equipping

Lord God,

It's easy to feel unprepared to write. There is so much to learn. There are so many other writers who could undoubtedly do it better.

But God, you promise that those you call to a task, you will also equip for that task. Thank you for how you've already prepared me to be a writer! How amazing to look back and realize that from a young age as I read stories, books, and poetry, you were already preparing my heart and mind to do this good work for you.

You've equipped me through experiences, study, and relationship with you, Lord. Thank you for the trials of my life that have pushed me to write and granted me insight into the human heart that I might connect to others through words.

I ask that you continue to equip me, Lord. Teach me ever more how I can improve my writing skills. But also Lord, equip me to share my words well, learning and effectively using all the other tools I will need to complete the call you've given me.

Amen

Scripture

1 Tim 3:16-17
All Scripture is breathed out by God and profitable for teaching, for reproof, for correction, and for training in righteousness, that the man of God may be complete, equipped for every good work.

Ephesians 4:11-12
And he gave the apostles, the prophets, the evangelists, the shepherds, and teachers to equip the saints for the work of ministry, for building up the body of Christ

Hebrews 13:20-21
Now may the God of peace [...] equip you with everything good that you may do his will.

Respond

Spend time thanking God for how he has already equipped you to be a writer.

_____
_____
_____
_____
_____
_____

How does trusting that God has equipped you change your feelings about your writing?

_____
_____
_____
_____
_____
_____
_____
_____
_____

Further study: Read 1 Samuel 16-24. How does the Lord equip David to be King? What trials in your life has he used to equip you?

_____
_____
_____
_____
_____
_____
_____
_____

In what area do you still feel ill-equipped? Ask the Lord to grow your skills and confidence in that area.

Priorities

Lord of All,

As the demands of work, family, friends, and writing all beg for my attention, I run to you for wisdom and guidance! Help me determine where to focus my time and energy.

If I stray from making my relationship with you my first and foremost, convict me of that idolatry and help me love you with all my heart, soul, mind and strength. Above all things, I place you as sovereign ruler and King.

I want to show up for what is important, Lord. So give me discipline to prioritize time with you, discipline to get enough sleep, and to prioritize my own wellbeing so I can give the other areas of my life my very best effort. When it feels impossible to do it all, help me know what to say no to so I can say yes to what matters most.

As I struggle with distractions from all the demands of my time, show me how to honor you in all that I do. Give me contentment in every season, as my momentary priorities must shift with the demands of life.

Amen

Scripture

Matthew 6:33
But seek first the kingdom of God and his righteousness, and all these things will be added to you.

Luke 12:34
For where your treasure is, there will your heart be also.

Deuteronomy 6:5
You shall love the Lord your God with all your heart and with all your soul and with all your might.

Respond

Is there anything you are placing above the Lord as your number one priority?

_____
_____
_____
_____
_____
_____
_____
_____

What areas do you want to prioritize more? What needs to change for you to live out your priorities?

___

Ask the Lord to help you determine and live out the priorities for your life. Where does writing fall on your priority list? Is that where you've been putting it?

Further Study: Read Luke 10:38-42. What does the story of Mary and Martha show us about proper priorities? How would Jesus react to how you spend your time and energy?

___

Personal Faith

Lord My God,

As I walk this road, there is nothing I hold more precious than my relationship with you. You are my rock, my redeemer, my ever-present help in trouble.

As I pour out into my writing, my family, my friendships, my work or my ministry... I never want to lose sight of your glory or the overwhelming beauty of a life spent in communion with you.

Lord, give me a heart that is chasing desperately after yours. Fill me with a hunger for your Word and your holy presence that cannot be quenched. When I stray from walking obediently in faith, I cling to your promise that you will never leave or forsake me. I rest in your unending love and merciful grace.

Let my faith be a faith that leaves a legacy for the generations, that leads people to you, and draws me ever closer to a glorious eternity in your presence.

Scripture

1 Peter 1:8-9

Though you have not seen him, you love him. Though you do not now see him, you believe in him and rejoice with joy that is inexpressible and filled with glory, obtaining the outcome of your faith, the salvation of your souls.

Ephesians 3:16-17a

I pray that out of his glorious riches he may strengthen you with power through his Spirit in your inner being, so that Christ may dwell in your hearts through faith.

Respond

Spend some time praising God for his
gift of salvation and faithfulness toward you.

_____
_____
_____
_____
_____
_____
_____
_____

What is hindering your walk with the Lord? Take time to confess your sins or express your doubts and call on God's faithfulness.

How does your personal faith impact the people around you? How does it impact your writing?

Magnificent God,

When I consider just how powerful, infinite, and holy you are, I cannot help but be brought to my knees. My insignificant human existence is but a wisp in your great plan.

You are the Lord of Hosts, the King of Kings, the Lord Most High. You created everything and only in you, everything remains.

Nothing else deserves my worship, Lord. Please, reveal any tendency within me to place anything above you in my heart or life. Whether it is my family, my work, my pleasure, or my pride... it is all filthy rags compared to your glory. Great and mighty is your name, O Lord!

My deepest desire is to worship you alone. Much like the songs of David, let my writing be an act of worship to you. Whatever genre I write, I submit every word as a heart offering to you, looking forward to the day when every knee will bow and heart declare you as Lord.

Scripture

Phillipians 2:10-11
That at the name of Jesus every knee should bow, of those in heaven, and of those on earth, and of those under the earth, and that every tongue should confess that Jesus Christ is Lord, to the glory of God the Father.

Revelation 4:11
You are worthy, our Lord and God, to receive glory and honor and power, for you created all things, and by your will they were created and have their being.

Psalm 146:1
You are worthy, our Lord and God, to receive glory and honor and power, for you created all things, and by your will they were created and have their being.

Respond

How has God revealed his glory and majesty to you lately? Did you praise him for it?

___
___
___
___
___
___

What are you tempted to worship above the Lord?

Further study: Read Psalm 150. How is your writing an expression of worship to the Lord?

Spend time meditating on the glory and majesty of the Lord. Declare his praise in your own words here.

_____
_____
_____
_____
_____
_____
_____
_____
_____
_____
_____
_____
_____
_____
_____
_____
_____
_____
_____
_____

PRAYER: FOR A WRITER'S HEART

Humility

Most High God,

It's so easy to fall into the trap of pride. If awards and accolades come, I pray I will never stop finding my validation and identity in my relationship with you.

As I work diligently to improve my craft, share my words, and become a successful writer, keep my heart focused on you. Let me never make the mistake of thinking that I am solely responsible for any measure of my success.

I want to always seek to lift up others and to serve my readers and other writers. Let my reputation as a writer be of kindness, humility, and compassion.

I want to be someone known for being "after God's own heart" just as King David was. Despite the power, money, reputation, and success he found, David sought after you in caves and in castles.

Whether I find worldly success as a writer or not, my sincerest desire is to serve you. Let me write to glorify not myself, but you, O Lord.

Amen

Scripture

Luke 14:11
For everyone who exalts himself will be humbled, and he who humbles himself will be exalted.

Philippians 2:3
Do nothing from rivalry or conceit, but in humility count others more significant than yourselves.

Colossians 3:12
Put on then, as God's chosen ones, holy and beloved, compassionate hearts, kindness, humility, meekness, and patience.

Respond

Godly humility is different from lack of confidence. Pray for God to increase your confidence in your writing while protecting you from a prideful spirit.

_____
_____
_____
_____
_____
_____
_____

Who are some examples of writers or people you view as humble and compassionate?

How can you serve other writers?

Spend some time examining your attitude and ego. Ask the Lord to correct any areas of need.

 Obedience

King of Kings,

I kneel before your throne, faced with the undeniable truth that you are Lord of all, sovereign and all powerful. And yet, you've given me free will to obey or not.

As a writer, I want to be obedient to that call on my life. If you call me to proclaim truth to a world that is confused, I need strength and courage.

Obedience might come at a cost, Lord. But I know that true obedience to you is always worthwhile. Recognizing you as ultimate ruler and lord of my life means that I will obey you. Even when it isn't easy.

Lord, help me be like the spiritual giants in your Word, who went where you instructed. Like the prophets who proclaimed your messages, however unpopular it would make them.

Help me determine when to write and when to remain silent, and graciously give me the exact spirit-led words for every situation. Whether the message is to be subtle or bold, let it be undeniably clear as I walk and write in obedience to your prompting.

Amen

Jeremiah 7:23
But this command I gave them: 'Obey my voice, and I will be your God, and you shall be my people. And walk in all the way that I command you, that it may be well with you.'

Psalm 143:10
Teach me to do your will, for you are my God! Let your good Spirit lead me on level ground!

Respond

Spend time asking the Lord to guide your writing.

_____
_____
_____
_____
_____
_____
_____
_____
_____
_____

Where have you seen blessing after obedience to God?

Obedience requires us to first listen to God's prompting. How can you leave space for God to speak into your writing?

Further Study: Read the book of Jonah. Is there a prompting you've been ignoring? Pray to God about how to be faithful in obedience.

My Heart

Jehovah-Raah (The Lord My Shepherd),

Jesus said that "out of the abundance of the heart, the mouth speaks" and I have to conclude that the same is true about the written word. It is out of the overflow of my heart that my words find their place on the page.

Help me protect my heart, O Lord. Show me how to guard it from the influence of a fallen world, and from the natural wickedness within me.

When I fall, draw me back to you and create in me a new heart! Show me any idol or treasure I hold that prevents me from loving you with all my heart, soul, mind and strength as you command.

Give me your heart for the people around me, that I might view them with compassion and kindness. May my heart be softened to your prompting, not hardened to my sin or to the darkness around me.

May the meditations of my heart be pleasing to you. Let my words be filled with light and life and hope, overflowing from a heart filled with your Holy Spirit.

Scripture

Luke 6:45
The good person out of the good treasure of his heart produces good, and the evil person out of his evil treasure produces evil, for out of the abundance of the heart his mouth speaks.

Psalm 19:14
Let the words of my mouth and the meditation of my heart be acceptable in your sight, O Lord, my rock and my redeemer.

Ezekiel 11:19
And I will give them one heart, and a new spirit I will put within them. I will remove the heart of stone from their flesh and give them a heart of flesh,

Respond

Spend some time praising the Lord for giving you a new heart with your salvation.

_____

_____

_____

_____

_____

_____

What is overflowing out of your heart
into your spoken and written words?

___

What does it look like to love the Lord with all your heart? How does that compare to your life?

Are there any areas of sin where your heart is hardened? Any place you lack compassion for others?

_____
_____
_____
_____
_____
_____
_____
_____
_____
_____
_____
_____
_____
_____
_____
_____
_____
_____
_____

Prayers for My Writing

"A word after a word after a word is power."

Margaret Atwood

Creativity

Creator God,

As I look at the world around me, I am awed by your creation. As I write, I strive to create beauty from nothingness, just as you did in the beginning.

As I'm writing, fill me with creativity that flows effortlessly, Father. Bring me ideas that glorify you, and reach hearts through new and innovative ways. Help me translate my thoughts to paper with clarity as well as beauty.

Let me never grow bored with the process of creation, but fill my creative well to overflowing, so ideas and excitement about each project pour out of me and onto the page.

Most of all, help me remember that I can only create because you first created me. Give me a new appreciation for how my creativity is a gift from you, my Creator.

You created me in your image, Lord, with a desire and an ability to create. Thank you for this wonderful gift!

Scripture

Genesis 1:1
*In the beginning, God created
the heavens and the earth.*

John 1:3
*All things were made through him, and
without him was not any thing made that was made.*

Genesis 1:27
*So God created man in his own image,
in the image of God he created him;
male and female he created them.*

Respond

Spend some time thanking the Lord for your creativity.

_____
_____
_____
_____
_____
_____
_____

What ideas are you excited about right now?

How can God the Creator inspire you as a creator?

What are you struggling with creatively?
Ask the Lord to meet you in your project.

PRAYERS FOR MY WRITING
Creating with God

Abba Father,

When I sit down to write, there is nothing I want more than for you to be sitting there with me. It's an honor to recognize that not only do you call me to write, and you equip me to write, but you sit with me in my project and inspire me.

What an amazing thought to explore, O God. You give me the desire to write, and I want to write for you. The idea that I can write with you is overwhelming and a bit foreign, Lord! What a time of togetherness and worship and communion with you.

As we write, give my words life, much as you give the Breath of Life to every person. Lord, I don't want to write without your presence and without your involvement.

Help me remember not to undertake any endeavor while trying to leave you on the sidelines. Your presence is with me, creating with me. I invite you into my writing, O Lord!

It is from you. It is for you. It is with you.

Scripture

1 Corinthians 3:16
Do you not know that you are God's temple and that God's Spirit dwells in you?

Psalm 90:17
Let the favor of the Lord our God be upon us, and establish the work of our hands upon us; yes, establish the work of our hands!

Respond

Spend some time thanking God for His presence while you write, creating alongside you.

___
___
___
___
___
___
___
___
___
___

Do you view God as an observer of
or an active participant in your writing?

How can you be more intentional to invite
God into your writing process?

How does viewing God as a writing partner change your perspective of your current project?

Boldness

Jehovah-Nissi (The Lord My Banner)

Writing is a scary thing, a bit like taking a piece of myself and sending it out into the world for others to despise or enjoy. It is worship and therapy and prayer and creativity, all wrapped up into one.

You've called me to be a writer, Lord. But sometimes, I feel so ill-prepared. I get nervous about what others will say. I am scared to share this piece of myself and hesitant to share the message you've placed on my heart.

But you've given me a spirit of boldness, not of fear! So Lord, give me courage to take the steps I am supposed to. Whether it is boldness to share my words with someone new, boldness to invest time or money I haven't before, boldness to write something I've been avoiding, or something else; help me know which step to take, and grant me the courage to act.

Like the Israelites who marched under your banner, I write under your banner. And your banner over me is love (Song of Sol 2:4). I can write confidently and boldly as I rest in your love.

Scripture

2 Timothy 1:7
*For God gave us a spirit not of fear
but of power and love and self-control.*

Ephesians 6:19-20
And also for me, that words may be given to me in opening my mouth boldly to proclaim the mystery of the gospel, for which I am an ambassador in chains, that I may declare it boldly, as I ought to speak.

1 John 4:18
There is no fear in love, but perfect love casts out fear. For fear has to do with punishment, and whoever fears has not been perfected in love.

Respond

Spend time thanking God for his banner of love.

_____
_____
_____
_____
_____
_____
_____

What does it look like for you to be bold in your writing?

In what area of your writing have you been fearful? Pray for the Lord to banish those fears and help you trust him.

Further Study: Read Acts 4:13-20.
What characteristics of Peter and John's boldness do you notice? Where does boldness come from?

Message

Creator God,

Your perfect Word stands through the ages, revealing your heart and touching lives with a perfectly inspired message. It seems a lofty goal, to impact people with mere words. I know, if I allow you to inspire my words, they too can touch hearts and lives.

As I write, O Lord, I want to craft my message carefully. I want people to leave the pages I've written taking something with them. Hope, joy, information, inspiration...All of these are noble goals, Lord.

May I be striving for the right message. If my ideas and goals don't align with yours for my writing, change my will to match yours. I may not be writing a sermon or something immediately recognized as faith-infused. But whatever my message or purpose may be, help me make sure it is the right one.

Help me convey my message effectively, Lord. Give me the words that are exactly the right ones to accomplish the purpose of my writing today. Let me be open to your prompting, divinely inspired to write not mere words, but words that will make an impact on the reader.

Scripture

Ecclesiastes 9:17
The words of the wise heard in quiet are better than the shouting of a ruler among fools.

Matthew 12:36
I tell you, on the day of judgment people will give account for every careless word they speak

Colossians 4:6
Let your speech always be gracious, seasoned with salt, so that you may know how you ought to answer each person.

Respond

Spend some time thanking the Lord for how he has or will use your words.

_____
_____
_____
_____
_____
_____
_____

What messages has Lord given you to share?

_____
_____
_____
_____
_____
_____
_____
_____
_____
_____

Do you struggle to share certain messages?
Ask the Lord for guidance and clarity.

_____
_____
_____
_____
_____
_____
_____
_____
_____
_____
_____

In addition to the message of our written words,
God calls us to be gracious in our speech.
Do your everyday words glorify the Lord?
Pray for self-control and conviction in this area.

Readers' Hearts

Divine Father,

As I am writing every word, you already know exactly who will read them. How amazing that you know the minute and the hour that those words will reach the hearts and minds of every single person! You know the very number of hairs on their heads.

Even as I am still writing some unfinished work, I praise you for how you are preparing the hearts of the readers I am writing for! I may not know them or their story. But I trust you to use my words.

The words I write may be for a thousand readers, or it may be for one reader. Whatever your intent, help me be satisfied with it. They may be readers one hundred years from now, or I may meet them tomorrow.

I submit this work to your hands. Prepare the hearts of those who will read these words so that they may be blessed by my obedience to you through the words I write.

Scripture

Isaiah 55:11
So shall my word be that goes out from my mouth; it shall not return to me empty, but it shall accomplish that which I purpose, and shall succeed in the thing for which I sent it.

Isaiah 14:27
For the Lord of hosts has purposed, and who will annul it? His hand is stretched out, and who will turn it back?

Respond

Spend some time thanking God for your future readers.

_____
_____
_____
_____
_____
_____
_____
_____
_____

How do you feel about knowing that God has already picked your future readers?

If your work touches one thousand lives or just one life... Do you feel differently about your success?

How do you hope your work impacts your readers? Pray a blessing over your work and their hearts.

Prayers for My Circle

"A book is simply the container of an idea—like a bottle; what is inside the book is what matters."

Angela Carter

My Partner

Lord Most High,

I am filled with gratitude for my partner. Thank you for creating them to be my perfect complement and for guiding our lives together.

Thank you for how they support my writing, in big and small ways. As I continue in this journey you've called me to, help us be united in our vision, priorities, and communication.

Help me to speak lovingly to my partner and respect the roles you have given each of us to fulfill uniquely. Let our partnership be a strong force for the Kingdom established here on earth and let our mutual love and sacrifice be an example of Christ's love for His bride, the church.

Where the enemy would seek to divide us, draw us ever closer. Tether us together so tightly we cannot be undone.

Show me how to be a supportive partner as well, how I can encourage them in the ways you have uniquely called them.

Amen

Scripture

Genesis 2:18
Then the Lord God said, "It is not good that the man should be alone; I will make him a helper fit for him."

1 Peter 4:8
Above all, keep loving one another earnestly, since love covers a multitude of sins.

Matthew 19.8
So they are no longer two but one flesh. What therefore God has joined together, let not man separate.

Respond

Spend time thanking God for your spouse. If you are unmarried, thank him for this season of singleness.

_____
_____
_____
_____
_____
_____
_____
_____

What impact does your writing have on your relationship? Likewise, what impact does your relationship have on your writing?

___

Where is God calling you to take steps toward your spouse in forgiveness, love, or communication?

Where is your writing a source of division for you and your spouse? Ask the Lord to unify you when it comes to your writing pursuits.

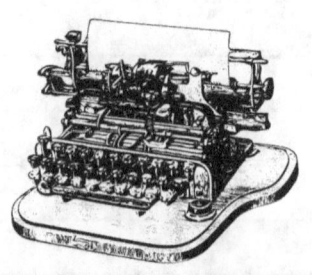

My Children

Father God,

Thank you for the gift of my children. Thank you for choosing imperfect, impatient me to be their parent.

Whether my kids ever read a word I write, I pray they recognize that pursuing something you are passionate about and obeying God's call is worthwhile. I pray they see me put you first, our family second, and everything else after.

I pray for their health, their hearts, and most importantly, their salvation. I desperately want them to know you, Lord! Help me teach them with grace and love, disciplining wisely when needed.

I pray that my writing would be a blessing to them, and never something that they come to resent.

Use my writing to make me a better parent. Help me be intentional with my time so I am fully present in moments with my family. Thank you for this outlet that is personal to me and my identity outside of that as a parent and caregiver.

Amen

Scripture

Psalm 127:3
*Behold, children are a heritage from the Lord,
the fruit of the womb a reward.*

Deuteronomy 6:6-7
And these words that I command you today shall be on your heart. You shall teach them diligently to your children, and shall talk of them when you sit in your house...and when you lie down, and when you rise.

Psalm 78:4
We will not hide them from their children, but tell to the coming generation the glorious deeds of the Lord, and his might, and the wonders that he has done.

Respond

Spend some time thanking God for your children.

_____
_____
_____
_____
_____
_____
_____

How does your writing affect your children?
How can it have a positive impact?

What do you hope your children learn
from your pursuit of writing?

What does it look like for you to prioritize your writing while still being a good, loving parent?
Ask God for help and guidance in this area.

_____
_____
_____
_____
_____
_____
_____
_____
_____
_____
_____
_____
_____
_____
_____
_____
_____

My Friendships

God Most High,

Thank you for my friendships. You have blessed me so abundantly with these people who know me intimately. I'm so grateful that I am not alone on this journey. Whether they have known me for one year or twenty, thank you for how you have intertwined our stories.

Lord, I praise you for the people you have brought alongside me to encourage, love, and inspire me in so many ways. As I meet new people, give me discernment on who my close friends should be.

I pray that you would step into any of my friendships where discord or tension remains, or where hurt or dishonesty hampers our relationship.

Help me to be a good friend: compassionate, generous, patient, and kind. I want to be a trustworthy confidant and a pointer to you in all things.

Scripture

1 Thessalonians 5:11
Therefore encourage one another and build one another up, just as you are doing.

Colossians 3:13
Bearing with one another and, if one has a complaint against another, forgiving each other; as the Lord has forgiven you, so you also must forgive.

Romans 12:10
Love one another with brotherly affection. Outdo one another in showing honor.

Respond

Spend time thanking the Lord for your friends, listing them by name.

_____
_____
_____
_____
_____
_____
_____

Are there friendships you need to attend to or forgiveness you need to seek or give?

How can you be intentional about investing in your friendships in the next week or two?

Ask the Lord for the protection of your friendships. If you lack close friends, ask the Lord to provide opportunities for new friendships to grow.

My Writer Friends

Father God,

Being a writer takes a special kind of person. Those who don't feel the urge to create pictures with words, tell stories, or pour their heart onto the page can never truly understand. So I thank you for the others I have met whom you created like me in this way.

Thank for the other writers who help me grow in my craft, encourage me when I feel distressed, and walk this often-lonely journey alongside me.

I'm so thankful for the wonder of technology, which allows me to connect with writers from around the world at the touch of a button, and for your divine provision in helping me make the right connections in a vast sea of writers.

Help me to be a good writing friend: honest, encouraging, and kind. Connect me with fellow writers who seek to honor you with their words the way I do.

Scripture

Proverbs 13:20
*Walk with the wise and become wise,
for a companion of fools suffers harm.*

Ecclesiastes 4:9-10
*Two are better than one, because they
have a good return for their labor:
If either of them falls down, one can help the other up.
But pity anyone who falls and
has no one to help them up.*

Respond

Spend time thanking God for any friendships
writing has brought into your life.

_____
_____
_____
_____
_____
_____
_____
_____

Ask the Lord to help you connect with other writers in your genre, location, or phase of journey.

_____
_____
_____
_____
_____
_____
_____
_____
_____

Where might the Lord be asking you to step out of your comfort zone to find or support writing friends?

_____
_____
_____
_____
_____
_____
_____
_____
_____
_____
_____

Why do you think it's important to have friends that share this part of your journey? Ask the Lord to provide friends that meet those specific needs.

___

My Teachers

God, my perfect teacher,

I seek instruction from many in this writing industry. Sometimes it is hard to recognize those who teach from greed or ambition, those who twist your words to suit their own purposes.

Grant me wisdom to discern the voices I should learn from and those I should ignore. Help me weed out the valuable instruction from the advice that would lead me down a path of disobedience, mistrust, or vain conceit in my writing and publishing journey.

Lord, bless those who teach me! Bless those who share their experience and wisdom openly, who rightly divide your Word, and who honestly seek to encourage and equip writers.

Thank you for the teachers I have learned from and will in the future as I grow as a writer. Guide me toward godly pastors and mentors who can speak your truth to me in all areas of life, including my writing.

Scripture

Luke 6:40
A disciple is not above his teacher, but everyone when he is fully trained will be like his teacher.

2 Timothy 4:3-4
For the time is coming when people will not endure sound teaching, but having itching ears they will accumulate for themselves teachers to suit their own passions, and will turn away from listening to the truth and wander off into myths.

Respond

Spend some time thanking God for your teachers, pastors, and mentors by name.

Have you experienced teachers who seem to have ulterior motives? How can you tell?

What qualities are important to you to find in a teacher? Ask the Lord to bring those teachers into your sphere.

Where do you feel your biggest need is
when it comes to teaching or mentoring?
Ask the Lord to fulfill that need with the right person.

My Writing Team

Father God,

As solitary a pursuit as writing is, I am easily tempted to try to do everything myself. Help me recognize that I cannot accomplish everything alone, and to choose wisely what I should do myself, and what I should outsource.

As I partner with designers, assistants, editors, or other businesses, help me ensure those partnerships are mutually beneficial.

Protect me from business transactions with those of questionable integrity. Lead me to those who I can trust, who will be reliable and do their work with pride and uphold high quality. I want to use my time and financial resources wisely, and my writing team is a big part of that.

Help me, in turn, be a creative person that others want to do business with: full of integrity, reliable, and proud of producing high quality work.

Amen

Scripture

Exodus 35:35
He has filled them with skill to do every sort of work done by an engraver or by a designer or by an embroiderer in blue and purple and scarlet yarns and fine twined linen, or by a weaver—by any sort of workman or skilled designer.

Psalm 112:5
It is well with the man who deals generously and lends; who conducts his affairs with justice.

Proverbs 28:6
Better is a poor man who walks in his integrity than a rich man who is crooked in his ways.

Respond

Spend time praying about your existing writing team.

_____
_____
_____
_____
_____
_____
_____

Have you invited others into your writing process? Are there places where you need to expand your team?

___

What qualities do you value in a business relationship? Ask the Lord to bring these kind of people to your writing team as needs arise.

___

Ask the Lord for protection of your business relationships. If you have none, ask for wisdom for when it may be time to expand your team.

My Prayer Team

Good and gracious Father,

You command us to pray continually in all things, and I as I pray over my writing, I also know that it is important enough for others to lift up as well.

Lord, bless those who pray on my behalf. Shower them with your abundant gifts and good favor! If I have not asked others to pray for my writing, give me courage to invite others to support me in this powerful way, being vulnerable about my need and my struggles so they can lift me up.

I thank you, good Father, for those who love me well and already join me in praying for my writing, as well as those who will in the future. There is no more powerful force on earth than that of prayer. And no better way to multiply the power than to be united in prayer with others.

Thank you for the gift of others who see the importance and value of my writing and who celebrate it with me, investing their time and hearts to lift it up to you.

Scripture

James 5:6
Therefore, confess your sins to one another and pray for one another, that you may be healed. The prayer of a righteous person has great power as it is working.

1 John 5:15
And if we know that he hears us in whatever we ask, we know that we have the requests that we have asked of him.

James 5:13-14
Is anyone among you suffering? Let him pray. Is anyone cheerful? Let him sing praise. Is anyone among you sick? Let him call for the elders of the church, and let them pray over him, anointing him with oil in the name of the Lord.

Respond

Spend time thanking God for the invitation to pray and the power of prayer.

_____
_____
_____
_____
_____

Who are prayer warriors in your life? How have you invited them to pray for your writing?

What could you do to start a team or grow the effectiveness of people who are praying for your writing?

What is your biggest prayer need right now? Have you communicated it to anyone?

Prayers for a Writing Career

"We are all apprentices in a craft where no one ever becomes a master."

Ernest Hemingway

Decisions

Almighty God,

As I walk this writing journey, I want to do so with wisdom, patience, and obedience. Lord, there are times when I am faced with many options. Multiple directions branch off in front of me like paths in the woods.

As I consider various decisions, I need your perfect guidance, lighting my steps through unfamiliar territory. If there are paths I should avoid, I would ask you to either close those doors, or make it clear to me that they are not for me. Speak to me through wise counsel, your Word, or your Holy Spirit, and give me ears and a heart to listen.

When I have made a decision, I ask for peace moving forward from it. That I wouldn't spend precious time looking backward to roads not taken. Help protect me by nudging me back to my own journey, when I might be tempted to focus too much on what someone else is doing.

Scripture

Proverbs 3:5-6
Trust in the Lord with all your heart, and do not lean on your own understanding. In all your ways acknowledge him, and he will make straight your paths.

Isaiah 30:21
And your ears shall hear a word behind you, saying, "This is the way, walk in it," when you turn to the right or when you turn to the left.

Proverbs 15:22
Without counsel plans fail, but with many advisers they succeed.

Respond

Spend some time thanking God for his guidance in your life.

Who do you seek godly counsel from when you have a decision to make? Thank the Lord for them, or ask for those relationships to grow.

Are there decisions you are looking back to, instead of focusing on the future? Lay them at the feet of Jesus and ask for peace.

What decision are you wrestling with right now?
Ask the Lord to give you wisdom about the choice.

Finances

Jehovah-Jireh (Lord My Provider)

In my writing, whether I aspire for it to be a profitable business or not, there will be some degree of financial ramification involved.

Lord, I submit my finances to you in every aspect, but especially my writing. Whether this art should generate financial blessing or not, the true blessing is in the reward of my obedience to you.

If my goal is to turn my writing into a business, then like any other business. Lord, I ask for guidance in financial decisions, protection from scammers or thieves, and your blessing over all my dealings.

Help me be a good steward of the resources you've given me. And Lord, if it is Your will, bless this business and my family financially, so I might serve you even more with those gifts.

Keep me from greed, Father. I know you are my ultimate provider, so help me find my security and peace in You, not earthly finances.

Scripture

Proverbs 28:25
*A greedy man stirs up strife, but the one
who trusts in the Lord will be enriched.*

Genesis 22:14
*So Abraham called the name of that place, "The Lord
will provide"; as it is said to this day,
"On the mount of the Lord it shall be provided."*

Matthew 6:19-21
*Do not lay up for yourselves treasures on earth, where
moth and rust destroy and where thieves break in and
steal, but lay up for yourselves treasures in heaven,
where neither moth nor rust destroys and where
thieves do not break in and steal. For where your
treasure is, there your heart will be also.*

Respond

Spend some time thanking the Lord for
the way he has blessed you financially.

_____
_____
_____
_____
_____

What does it mean to trust the Lord with the financial aspect of your writing?

What does it meant to you to write in confidence of the Lord as your Jehovah-Jireh?

What kind of financial goals do you have for your business? How can you pursue these goals diligently, while still holding your writing with an open hand?

___

PRAYERS FOR A WRITING CAREER:

Good Father,

I know that what the world calls success often finds men empty and discouraged. It's easy to fall into the trap of seeking fame, money, or acclaim, thinking that these things will satisfy.

None of these things are inherently bad, Father, but I never want to place them in importance above obedience or my walk with you. True satisfaction is found in you, when strivings cease.

Lord, help me to define success the way you do. A life well-lived, running the race set before me. Help me consider my success to be when I stand before you and hear "Well done, my good and faithful servant." What a marvelous day that will be, O Lord!

As you bless my writing, I may receive worldly success also. Help my heart to remain focused on you. Where I have found earthly success, I give you the glory, for I owe everything to you!

I never want to measure my success against someone else's, constantly comparing and consumed with envy. Guard my heart against such things and turn it ever toward you, Lord.

Scripture

James 4:10
*Humble yourselves before the Lord,
and he will exalt you.*

Matthew 16:26
*For what will it profit a man if he gains the
whole world and forfeits his soul?
Or what shall a man give in return for his soul?*

Matthew 6:33
*But seek first the kingdom of God and his
righteousness, and all these things
will be added to you.*

Respond

Spend time praising God for how
he has blessed your writing.

___
___
___
___
___
___
___
___

What earthly measures of success are you most likely to strive for? Pray for God to guard your heart against that temptation.

___

What will it be like to hear God say these words? "Well done, my good and faithful servant." You may choose to write a scene, poem, or song.

How do you define success?
Does it match with how God defines success?
Pray for alignment in those definitions, keeping
in mind that it will not be God who changes.

PRAYERS FOR A WRITING CAREER: Platform

Lord Most High,

Along with my words, you've given me the ability to share them. Whether that is with two people or two million people, I desperately want my words to impact them.

Whether I share my words online or in person, I'm trusting you to help my words find the audience they are meant for.

Keep me from falling into the trap of finding my validation from the size of my platform or trying to make my name great. At the same time, I ask you to grow my platform by bringing the right audience to my circle.

It's easy to get caught up in numbers, especially in the competitive world of publishing. But I recognize that each follower, reader, or subscriber is a living, breathing child of yours. Help me to value each and every one. Show me how to not only grow this platform, but how to use use it effectively and engage authentically.

Scripture

John 12:43
For they loved the glory that comes from man more than the glory that comes from God.

Galatians 1:10
For am I now seeking the approval of man, or of God? Or am I trying to please man? If I were still trying to please man, I would not be a servant of Christ.

John 5:44
How can you believe, when you receive glory from one another and do not seek the glory that comes from the only God?

Respond

Spend some time thanking God for those you get to share your writing with: the two or the two million!

_____
_____
_____
_____
_____
_____
_____
_____

What sort of pressure do you feel to grow your platform? What truths do you need to remember about your platform?

_____
_____
_____
_____
_____
_____
_____

Write a prayer of submission regarding your platform and audience size to the Lord.

_____
_____
_____
_____
_____
_____
_____
_____
_____
_____

Pray for God's abundant blessing on your platform. Ask Him to guide your interactions and bring the right people into your sphere of influence.

Reputation

Lord my Protector,

As a creator and business-person, integrity is of the utmost importance. Help me to be a person of unquestionable character, honest in all my dealings and someone who people admire.

Let me be someone people want to work and partner with, endorse, or support.

In secular circles, let me be known as a strong believer: firm in my convictions, but gracious and loving to those who don't believe as I do.

Let me be a light for you in dark places, as well as an upright example for other believers in Christian circles.

Lastly, Lord, protect me from anyone with slanderous intent or destructive motives who would damage my reputation for their own selfish gain or nefarious pleasure. Guard my business from trolls, scammers, cheats, or imposters with your divine hand.

Scripture

1 Timothy 4:12
Let no one despise you[...], but set the believers an example in speech, in conduct, in love, in faith, in purity.

Proverbs 22:1
A good name is to be chosen rather than great riches, and favor is better than silver or gold.

Respond

Think about people you admire and their reputation. What aspects are important to you? Ask God to multiply those in you.

_____
_____
_____
_____
_____
_____
_____
_____
_____
_____

What does it mean for you to act with integrity in all aspects of your business?

In our world, your reputation could come under fire at any time, through no fault of your own. Ask the Lord to protect you from those kinds of attacks.

Do you need to adjust any behavior where you haven't been acting with integrity? Are you a light for nonbelievers in your words and deeds?

___

Technology

Sovereign Lord of All,

It's amazing how much of my writing and business relies on technology. Such tools are both a blessing and a source of trouble.

Lord, even the smallest piece of our universe is not beyond your control. This includes the clouds, codes, algorithms, hardware, or software we rely on in so many ways.

I ask your divine blessing over the technology I rely on. Protect my data from destruction or attack. Grant me relief from frustration that might rise through errors, glitches, or algorithmic changes. Be gracious to me in this, allowing all the systems to work as intended when I need to them.

When I need to learn, give me a teachable heart and a nimble mind that can grasp new technological concepts in order to further my writing and business.

Scripture

Psalm 135:6
Whatever the Lord pleases, he does, in heaven and on earth, in the seas and all deeps.

Daniel 2:21
He changes times and seasons; he removes kings and sets up kings; he gives wisdom to the wise and knowledge to those who have understanding

Job 42:2
I know that you can do all things, and that no purpose of yours can be thwarted.

Respond

Spend some time thanking God for how technology is a positive contribution to your writing.

_____
_____
_____
_____
_____
_____
_____
_____

What areas of technology provide the most frustration for you? Pray over those areas.

___

How does God's sovereignty impact your attitude about technology. Do you believe he is in control of even technological things?

What is an upcoming or ongoing area of technological reliance for you? Pray a special blessing over that specific task or requirement.

Opportunities

Lord Most High,

As I strive to write for you, in worship and obedience and joyful celebration of how you've created me, I recognize that opportunities of all kinds may find me.

When I am faced with an opportunity, help me decide whether to take it, knowing my heart and goals for my writing, guide my decisions in those times.

Bring the right opportunities to me Lord. I ask you to open doors I never thought possible, giving me the confidence to embrace opportunities that are a gift from you.

Give me contentment with the opportunities I have to share my writing. Keep me from coveting the seat at a table to which I haven't been invited. Help me trust that you will bring the right opportunities to me at the right time.

And when opportunity strikes, give me the peace and confidence to grab hold, not wasting time or worrying, but not rushing into anything too quickly.

Scripture

Proverbs 16:9
The heart of man plans his way, but the Lord establishes his steps.

Jeremiah 29:11
For I know the plans I have for you, declares the Lord, plans for welfare and not for evil, to give you a future and a hope.

Psalm 32:8
I will instruct you and teach you in the way you should go; I will counsel you with my eye upon you.

Respond

Spend time thanking God for the opportunities He's given you.

_____

_____

_____

_____

_____

_____

_____

What opportunities are on the horizon for you right now? Pray about them.

Are you chasing opportunities too hard, trusting the Lord to bring them to you in his time, or holding back from saying yes to something?

What opportunity do you hope presents itself in the future? Pray about that opportunity and ask for direction and patience.

Time Management

Lord God,

In the busyness of life, writing sometimes feels like a desperately needed reprieve. Other times, with the addition of deadlines or expectations, it can become another task on the endless to-do list.

Father, help me use my time wisely to accomplish all that you have laid out before me to do. Multiply my moments, capturing pockets of time to your glory that I might otherwise wither away.

Free me from habitual time-wasters and addictions to social or other media. Teach me to number my days, and hours and minutes, wisely.

Help me to work hard, so that I may rest well. For rest without work is laziness, while work without rest leads to dissatisfaction and soul-weariness. Neither of which is your desire or plan for me.

Let me never neglect taking my time with you, Lord. I treasure these moments with you, and time spent in your presence is never wasted.

Scripture

Psalm 90:12
*So teach us to number our days
that we may get a heart of wisdom.*

Proverbs 6:6-8
*Go to the ant, O sluggard;
consider her ways, and be wise.
Without having any chief, officer, or ruler,
she prepares her bread in summer
and gathers her food in harvest.*

Ephesians 5:15-17
*Look carefully then how you walk, not as unwise
but as wise, making the best use of the time,
because the days are evil.*

Respond

Spend time in worship of the Lord.
Thank him for giving you today and every day.

___
___
___
___
___
___

How does your time reflect your values?

Do you feel like you have enough time to accomplish everything you need to, while still having time to rest?

In what areas does your time-management need adjusted? Ask the Lord to help you break bad habits, form new ones and rely on him for the time and energy to work diligently.

Prayers for Specific Times

"Fill your paper with the breathings of your heart."

— William Wordsworth

Morning Writing

Good Father,

This morning, I come with humble expectation. That you will meet me here, in the newness of the day as I sit to write. As the rest of the world sleeps or starts their day, I come to write, answering the call you've given me.

Energize me for this work, Lord, though I may still feel tired from yesterday's work, or in anticipation of the the day to come. Help me set aside what will come later, so I can use this time to create, Father.

Give me clarity of thought and multiply my time, Lord. Let the words flow through me, as though being penned by your very own hand.

Thank you, O Lord, for being here with me. Thank you for your mercies new every morning.

Psalm 90:14
*Satisfy us in the morning with your steadfast love,
that we may rejoice and be glad all our days.*

PRAYERS FOR SPECIFIC TIMES

Morning Writing

Psalm 90:14
*Satisfy us in the morning with your steadfast love,
that we may rejoice and be glad all our days.*

Afternoon Writing

Almighty Savior,

Much of the day has come and gone. I've surely stumbled more than once as I've gone about my day. I confess to you my failures and ask your forgiveness.

As I sit down to write this afternoon, energize me, O Lord! My tired bones already long for the comfort of rest at day's end, but that time is not yet here. Give me stamina and fortitude as the afternoon minutes pass by.

I offer this time to you. Meet me in the pages and help me focus my wandering thoughts. Keep me from distractions, either self-inflicted or from others.

Whether this is children's naptime or my lunch break or another quiet time, thank you for this opportunity to write. Bless this time and help me to treasure it and use it wisely.

Isaiah 40:31
They who wait for the Lord shall renew their strength; they shall mount up with wings like eagles; they shall run and not be weary; they shall walk and not faint.

PRAYERS FOR SPECIFIC TIMES
Afternoon Writing

Amen

Isaiah 40:31
They who wait for the Lord shall renew their strength; they shall mount up with wings like eagles; they shall run and not be weary; they shall walk and not faint.

Evening Writing

Lord God,

As the day draws to a close, I am so tempted to use this time for other things. There is a list of uncompleted tasks I could attend to. I could choose to claim some needed relaxation with a book or a movie. I am tempted to waste away the time before bed on my phone or with another non-priority.

I am tired from the day, eager for my bed and the peaceful rest of sleep.

But here I am, Lord. I offer this time to you, with expectant hope that you will meet me here. Energize me for the work ahead. Fill me with creativity, motivation, and fortitude to pour out my thoughts on paper. As the hour grows late, multiply this time with a supernatural hand, allowing me to write more than I could imagine.

Thank you for this time to dedicate to you and to my writing, when children slumber and the lights are dimmed. I praise you for the opportunity to write tonight. Rest will come later.

Psalm 8:3-4
When I look at your heavens, the work of your fingers, the moon and the stars, which you have set in place, what is man that you are mindful of him, and the son of man that you care for him?

PRAYERS FOR SPECIFIC TIMES
Evening Writing

Psalm 8:3-4
When I look at your heavens, the work of your fingers, the moon and the stars, which you have set in place, what is man that you are mindful of him, and the son of man that you care for him?

Publication

Great and Magnificent Father,

Praise you to the highest heavens! To you be all the glory and power and honor forever and ever, O Lord. You are sovereign above all things and I worship you.

How amazing to have something I wrote out in the world for people to read! Thank you for allowing me to fulfill your calling, for blessing these words during the writing. Thank you for directing the opportunity for them to find their way into the world. I know that the way these words were published is exactly how you intended.

And now, I offer them to you, Lord. As the writer, I have done my part. While I may spread the word, marketing and promoting, everything that happens from here is out of my control. Take these words and direct their path to the readers who need them.

If you send them to one million readers, then I will praise you. If only one reader finds them, I will praise you. If I get rave reviews, I give you the glory. If the reviews are critical, I rest in my effort and my obedience to you.

Psalm 71:8
My mouth is filled with your praise,
and with your glory all the day.

PRAYERS FOR SPECIFIC TIMES

Publication

Psalm 71:8
*My mouth is filled with your praise,
and with your glory all the day.*

Creator God,  Beginning

The empty page sits before me, full of possibilities. Like you, in the beginning, created order from the chaos, I attempt to do the same. It is an intimidating prospect, to create something from nothing.

Sometimes, a blank page carries apprehension, as I focus on the end before I've even begun. Help me quiet any thoughts of anxiety and simply enjoy the process, remembering that You are here with me in the writing.

Remind me of the joy of writing as I begin this new work. You made me a writer, Lord. Thank you for this opportunity to write something new.

Lord, throughout this project, whether it takes minutes or years to complete, guide my steps and my words. Help me write the words meant for the readers down the line. Use this process to draw me closer to you, let it be an act of worship and creativity and prayer, all in one.

I offer this new page to you.

Isaiah 43:19
Behold, I am doing a new thing; now it springs forth, do you not perceive it? I will make a way in the wilderness and rivers in the desert.

PRAYERS FOR SPECIFIC TIMES

Beginning

Amen

Isaiah 43:19
Behold, I am doing a new thing; now it springs forth, do you not perceive it? I will make a way in the wilderness and rivers in the desert.

Writer's Block

Good and gracious Father,

I'm stuck, Lord. I need your divine power to overcome this obstacle!

Give me clarity where there is only confusion. If the problem is with my project and I don't know what to write now, grant me the divine inspiration for what comes next!

Give me motivation where there is only resistance. If the problem is with my desire to write, fill me with a renewed sense of passion and eagerness to fill the page with new words.

Give me words that flow like steady streams where there is only a small trickle. If the problem is with choosing words, paralyzed with the importance of choosing the exact right ones, or the inability to find the words I am searching for, unblock the dam and let the words flow. Give me the peace to write the not-quite-right word for now, and come back to it later.

And if I need to rest and wait, give me peace to do so.

James 1:12
Blessed is the man who remains steadfast
under trial, for when he has stood the test
he will receive the crown of life, which God
has promised to those who love him.

PRAYERS FOR SPECIFIC TIMES

Writer's Block

James 1:12
Blessed is the man who remains steadfast under trial, for when he has stood the test he will receive the crown of life, which God has promised to those who love him.

Editing

Perfect God,

Thank you for this time and opportunity to carefully consider the words of my writing. How I wish I could so carefully consider the words I speak before they were said!

Editing is a daunting task, Lord. Give me patience and fortitude for the process. Allow me to see my writing in a new way, with fresh eyes to catch every mistake or unclear thought. Let the needed changes light up before my eyes, divinely highlighted by you, my co-creator! And then, show me just how to change things to complete this work to the very best of my ability.

But also, give me the peace to accept that I am not perfect, nor will anything that I create be. You are the only perfect creator, God. When it is time to release my work into the world, allow me to do so without anxiety or stressing about imperfection.

Help me be diligent, but not obsessive in my editing.

Psalm 18:30
This God—his way is perfect;
the word of the Lord proves true; he is a
shield for all those who take refuge in him.

PRAYERS FOR SPECIFIC TIMES

Editing

Amen

Psalm 18:30
This God—his way is perfect;
the word of the Lord proves true; he is a
shield for all those who take refuge in him.

Finishing a Project

Good Father,

Oh, how you must have felt at the end of the sixth day of Creation! To look at your creation and say "It is good!"

Thank you for allowing me a glimpse of that feeling, as I finish this project, I praise you as my creator, sustainer, guide, and savior. Thank you for the inspiration for the project, and the ways you helped me bring it to completion.

Thank you for walking beside me every step of the way. I'm sorry for the times I shut you out, resisted your guiding hand, or tried to force my own way.

Show me what comes next for this piece of writing, Lord. Make it clear how and when to share it with the world, if I am to do so.

But for now, Lord, help me rest as you did on the seventh day.

Genesis 2:3
So God blessed the seventh day and made it holy,
because on it God rested from all his
work that he had done in creation.

PRAYERS FOR SPECIFIC TIMES

Finishing a Project

Amen

Genesis 2:3
So God blessed the seventh day and made it holy,
because on it God rested from all his
work that he had done in creation.

Rejection and Criticism

Jehovah-Shalom (Lord My Peace),

My heart is hurting right now with the sharp sting of rejection or criticism. It is hard to put myself out there over and over again, only to be disappointed.

I don't understand, and I may never understand. But I trust that you have a plan for me and my writing. Help me to rest in your plan and your peace.

When you send encouragement amidst the setbacks, give me ears to hear those, as you speak through my friends and teachers.

If I am walking down roads or attempting to go through doors you do not desire for me, please show me the way to go instead.

If this rejection is part of the plan, then give me perseverance to continue despite the trials. Grant me a deep assurance within that you are with me, walking alongside me in the valleys of rejection and hurt. Banish any doubts from my mind about my abilities or my calling that this criticism stirs up.

Romans 15:13
May the God of hope fill you with all joy and peace in believing, so that by the power of the Holy Spirit you may abound in hope.

Rejection and Criticism

PRAYERS FOR SPECIFIC TIMES

Romans 15:13
May the God of hope fill you with all joy and peace in believing, so that by the power of the Holy Spirit you may abound in hope.

Anxiety

Jehovah-Shalom (Lord My Peace),

I need your perfect peace to calm my trouble soul, Lord. I trust your plan for me and my writing, but these anxious thoughts chase me. Relentless thoughts about the "what ifs" I cannot control have me pre-occupied and restless, spiraling in negative thoughts about the unknowns. My fears assail me, and I cling to you against the torrent of my anxiety.

But you are the comforter to the troubled, Lord! I call on your name now, in this very moment. Give me strength and a clear mind, that I might rest in your provision, your plan, and your amazing power, O God. Grant me relief from these anxious thoughts, quiet my soul, and engulf me in your perfect peace. Despite the unknowns in my current circumstance, I trust in you. You are bigger than every unknown, every fear, and every worry.

Help me to take every thought captive, Lord! I want to concentrate on everything that is noble and true. Grant me peace in the waiting, strengthening my faith in this trial as your Word promises you will.

Philippians 4:6-7
Do not be anxious about anything, but in everything by prayer and supplication with thanksgiving let your requests be made known to God. And the peace of God, which surpasses all understanding, will guard your hearts and your minds in Christ Jesus.

PRAYERS FOR SPECIFIC TIMES

Anxiety

Philippians 4:6-7
Do not be anxious about anything, but in everything by prayer and supplication with thanksgiving let your requests be made known to God. And the peace of God, which surpasses all understanding, will guard your hearts and your minds in Christ Jesus.

Waiting

Lord God,

It's impossible for me to comprehend how you exist outside of our human time. You are not bound by this construct of minutes and hours and days that you created for us. And right now, Lord, these minutes feel like days and the days stretch as though they are months.

I'm here waiting, Lord! I don't want to be discouraged or doubt you while I'm waiting for you to move. Remind me of the confidence I have in you and forgive my impatience as I fail to trust fully in your perfect timing. Thank you for meeting and sitting with me in the waiting.

Thank you for the gracious reminders of your sovereignty in this season. Open my eyes and heart to receive those messages of encouragement while I wait, and show me how to honor you and trust you in the midst of waiting.

As you work in the background now for your purposes, help me rest in your peace.

Isaiah 40:31
But they who wait for the Lord shall
renew their strength; they shall mount up with
wings like eagles; they shall run and not be weary;
they shall walk and not faint.

PRAYERS FOR SPECIFIC TIMES

Waiting

Isaiah 40:31
But they who wait for the Lord shall renew their strength; they shall mount up with wings like eagles; they shall run and not be weary; they shall walk and not faint.

Comparison

Lover of My Soul,

How easily I fall into the trap of comparing myself with others! Instead of trusting you and focusing on the race set before me, I look left or right. My heart twinges with bitterness and envy, instead of reveling with joy in the gifts and wonder of all you've given to me.

Forgive me, Father, for my ungrateful heart! Help me focus on you and what you have called me to do. When I am tempted to squeeze into tables I wasn't invited to, remind me to let you guide my steps. When I'm allowing the success of others determine my feelings of value or accomplishment, remind me of your steadfast love, perfect timing, and boundless grace.

When I'm too caught up in jealousy of the progress or success of others to spur them on in encouragement, convict my spirit and refine me to pure silver, Lord. Help me be truly satisfied with you and you alone. You have given me everything I need and abundantly more. My cup overflows with blessings! I praise you now and forever.

1 Timothy 6:6-7
But godliness with contentment is great gain, for we brought nothing into the world, and we cannot take anything out of the world.

PRAYERS FOR SPECIFIC TIMES

Comparison

1 Timothy 6:6-7
But godliness with contentment is great gain, for we brought nothing into the world, and we cannot take anything out of the world.

Dear God

ADDITIONAL PRAYERS

Dear God

Amen

Next Steps

Thank you for joining me on this journey of prayer and reflection. I never intended this to be a book available to the public. As a gift to some of my closest writing friends, I hoped to put into words some of the prayers I offered to the Lord for my own writing and business.

What I found was an entire community of writers hungry for guidance on how to pray for their writing and an easy-to-use place to explore the relationship between their faith and their craft.

I hope this book was a blessing to you. And I hope you come back to these prayers again and again as I do, for in different seasons each topic will strike your heart differently. The Spirit will speak to you in new ways each time.

I'd be honored if you'd leave a review for this book on Amazon or wherever you purchased it. If you have writing friends who would enjoy it, please consider a personal recommendation or gift. Prayer is a powerful tool for every writer.

You can learn more about additional author resources at The Inspired Author website.

The Inspired Author
www.TheInspiredAuthor.net

About the Author

Tara Grace Ericson is an award-winning author of Christian romance and romantic suspense. Her stories of faith, hope, and happily ever after connect with readers from all walks of life with their memorable characters and uplifting plots. Tara lives in the Ozarks as a stay-at-home mom to her three boys and is married to her favorite romantic hero: her husband of more than twelve years.

Learn more about Tara's fiction books at her website.

www.taragraceericson.com

Tara is also the co-founder of The Inspired Author, a platform dedicated to developing resources for excellence in writing craft and encouragement of Christian writers.

Sign up for The Inspired Author email list to receive encouragement for Christian writers as well as updates on books, courses, and more.

www.ingramcontent.com/pod-product-compliance
Lightning Source LLC
Chambersburg PA
CBHW070143080526
44586CB00015B/1820